DOMITILLE DE PRESSENSÉ

Emily's House

KINGFISHER BOOKS

Kingfisher Books, Grisewood & Dempsey Ltd,
Elsley House, 24-30 Great Titchfield Street,
London W1P 7AD

First published in this edition in the UK
in 1989 by Kingfisher Books
Originally published in France in 1985 by
Rouge et Or under the title La Maison D'Émilie

Copyright © Rouge et Or 1985
Copyright © in this translation Grisewood & Dempsey Ltd 1989

All rights reserved. No part of this publication
may be reproduced, stored in a retrieval system or
transmitted by any means, electronic, mechanical,
photocopying or otherwise, without the prior
permission of the publisher.

BRITISH LIBRARY CATALOGUING IN PUBLICATION DATA
De Pressensé, Domitille
  Emily's House. — 2nd
  1. English language. Readers — For children
  I. Title II. La maison d'Émilie. *English*
  428.6
  ISBN 0 86272 487 2

Translated by Philip Gibbs
Edited by Jackie Dobbyne
Phototypeset by Turner Typesetting
Printed in Spain

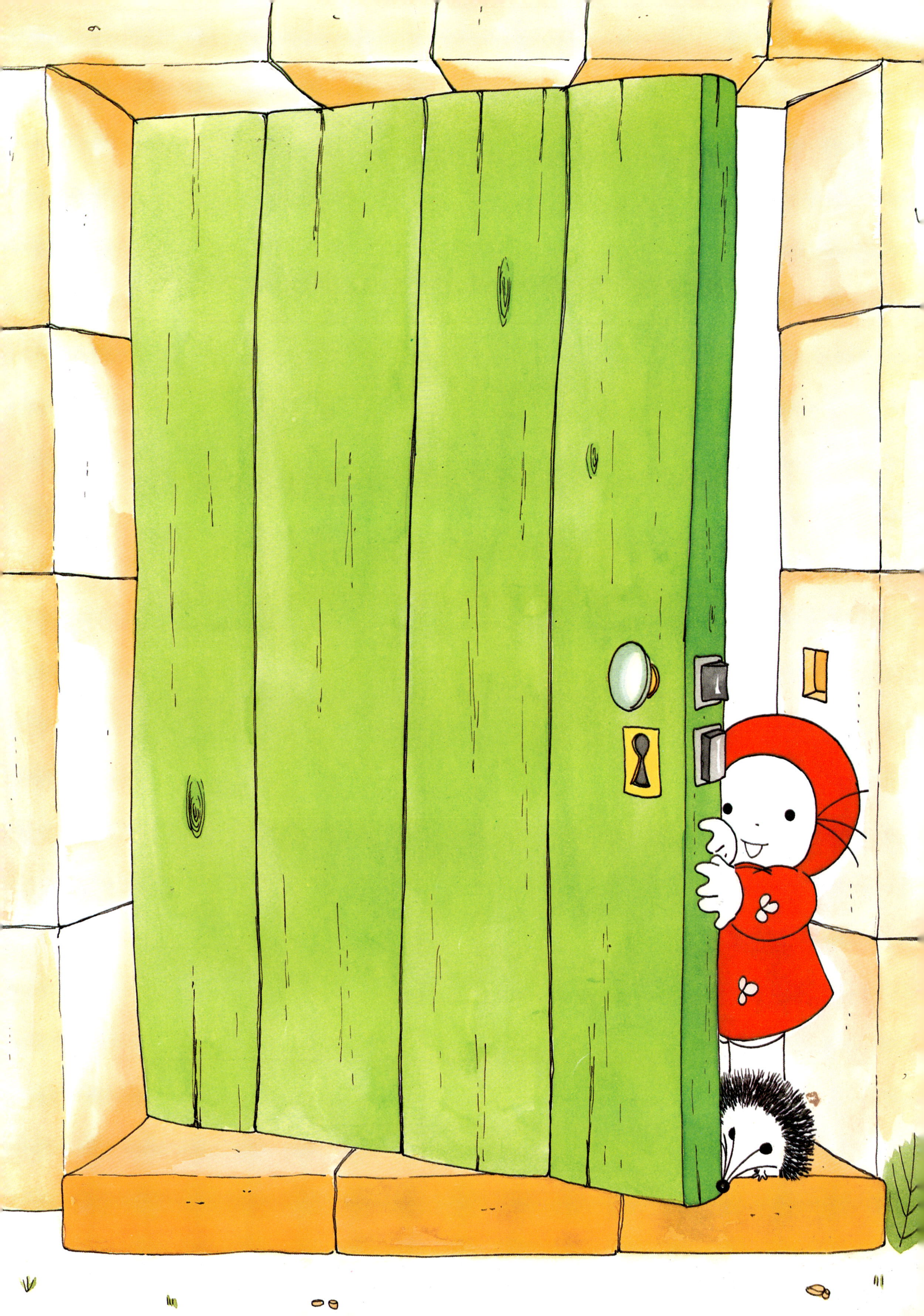

Hooray! I've got a torch!	It's mine. My very own.
Harriet gave it to me.	I think it could be a magic torch.

I am going to explore the whole house.

Daddy says: You know, Emily, it isn't a toy. If you keep switching it on and off the batteries will wear out and the torch won't work when you need it tonight.

Oh, I know that, Daddy.
Come on, Stephen. Let's go.

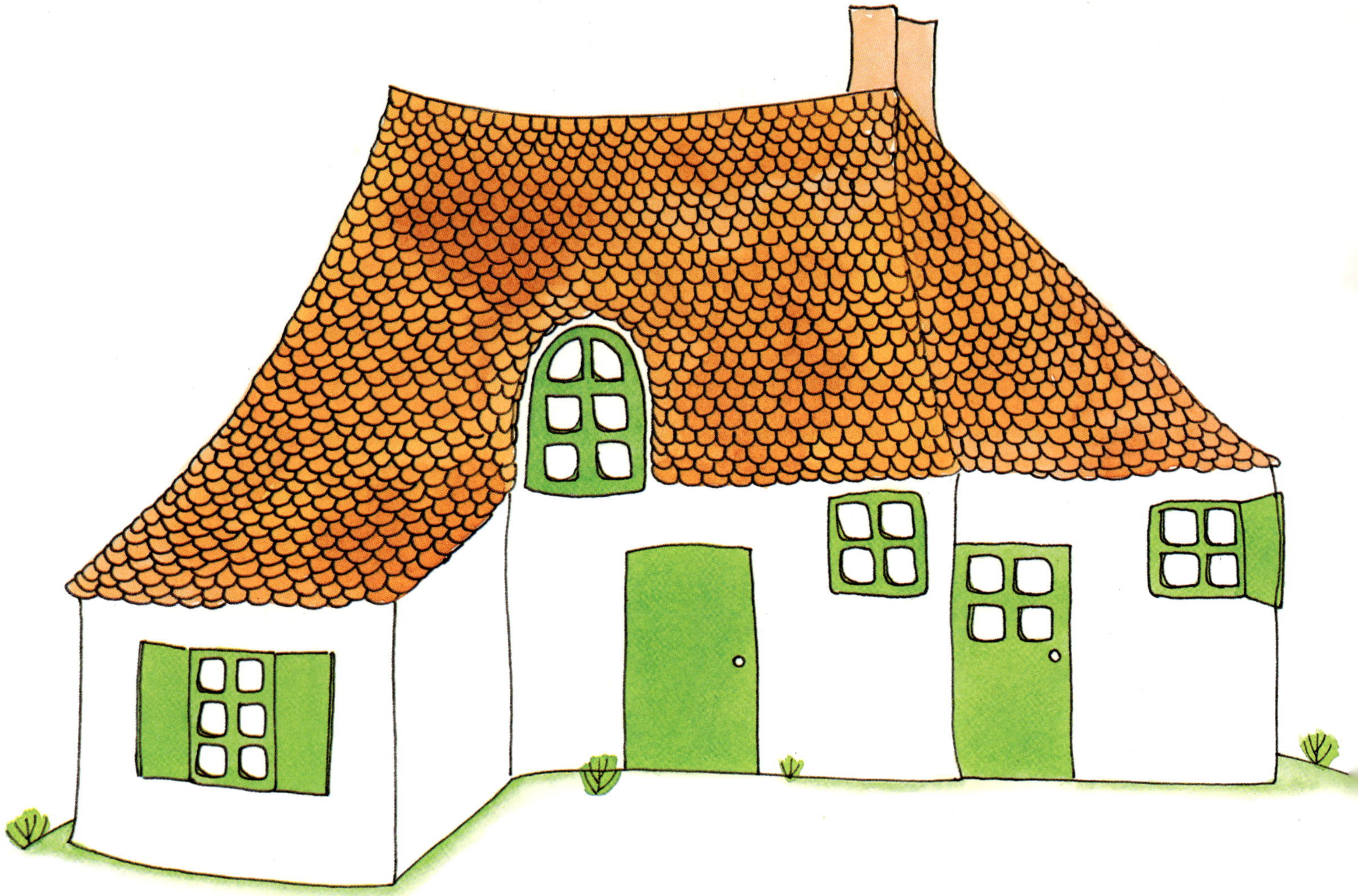

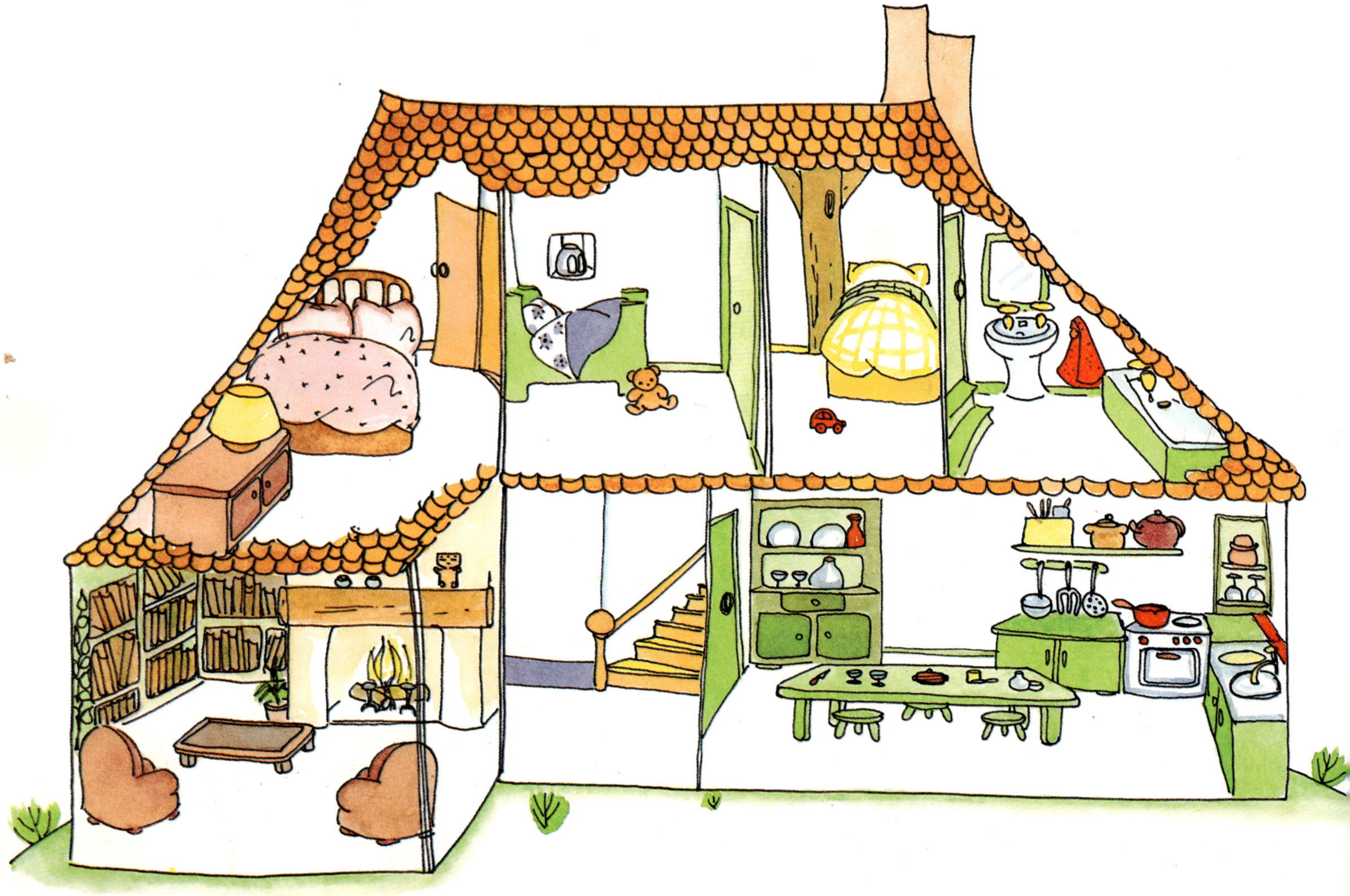

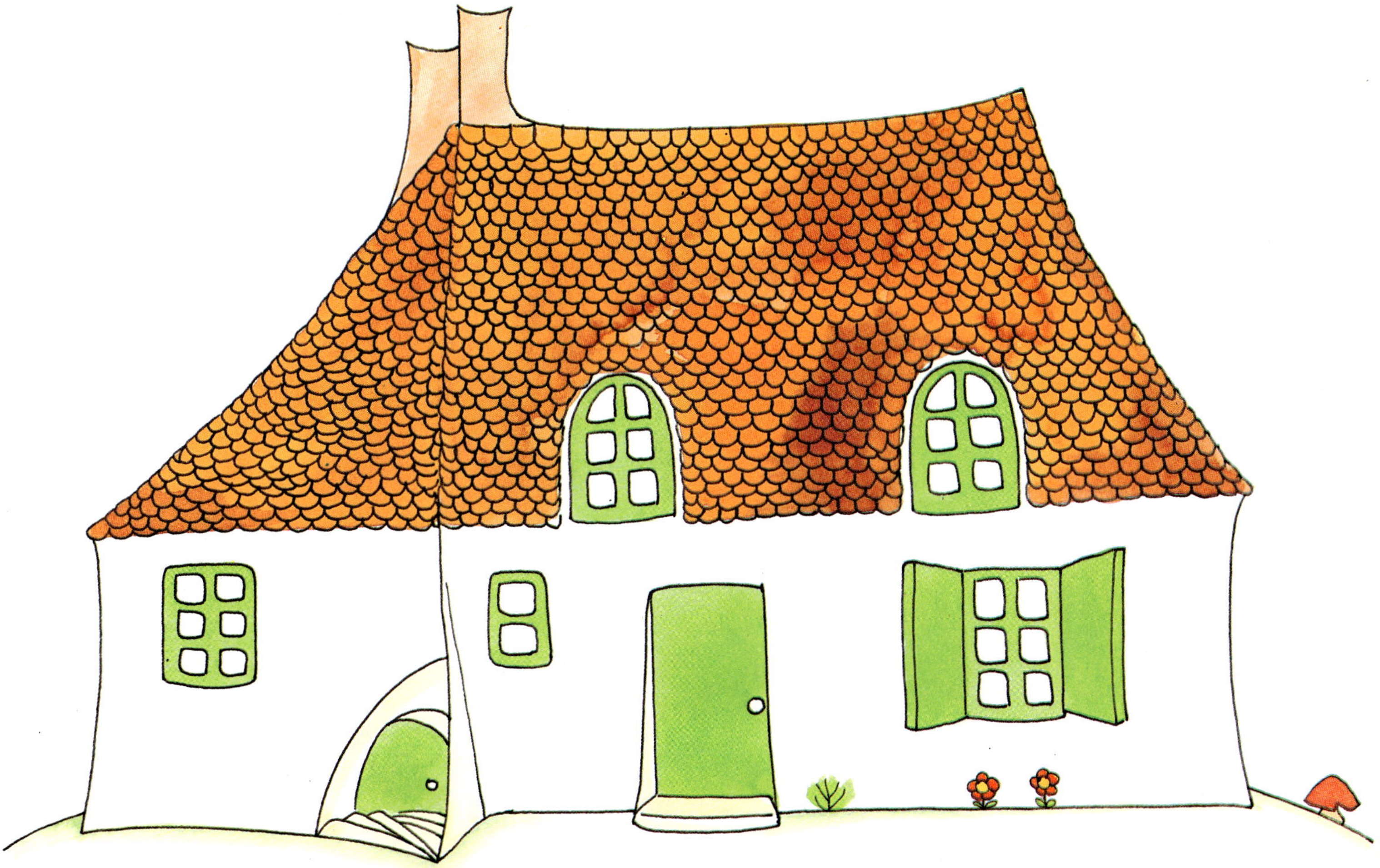

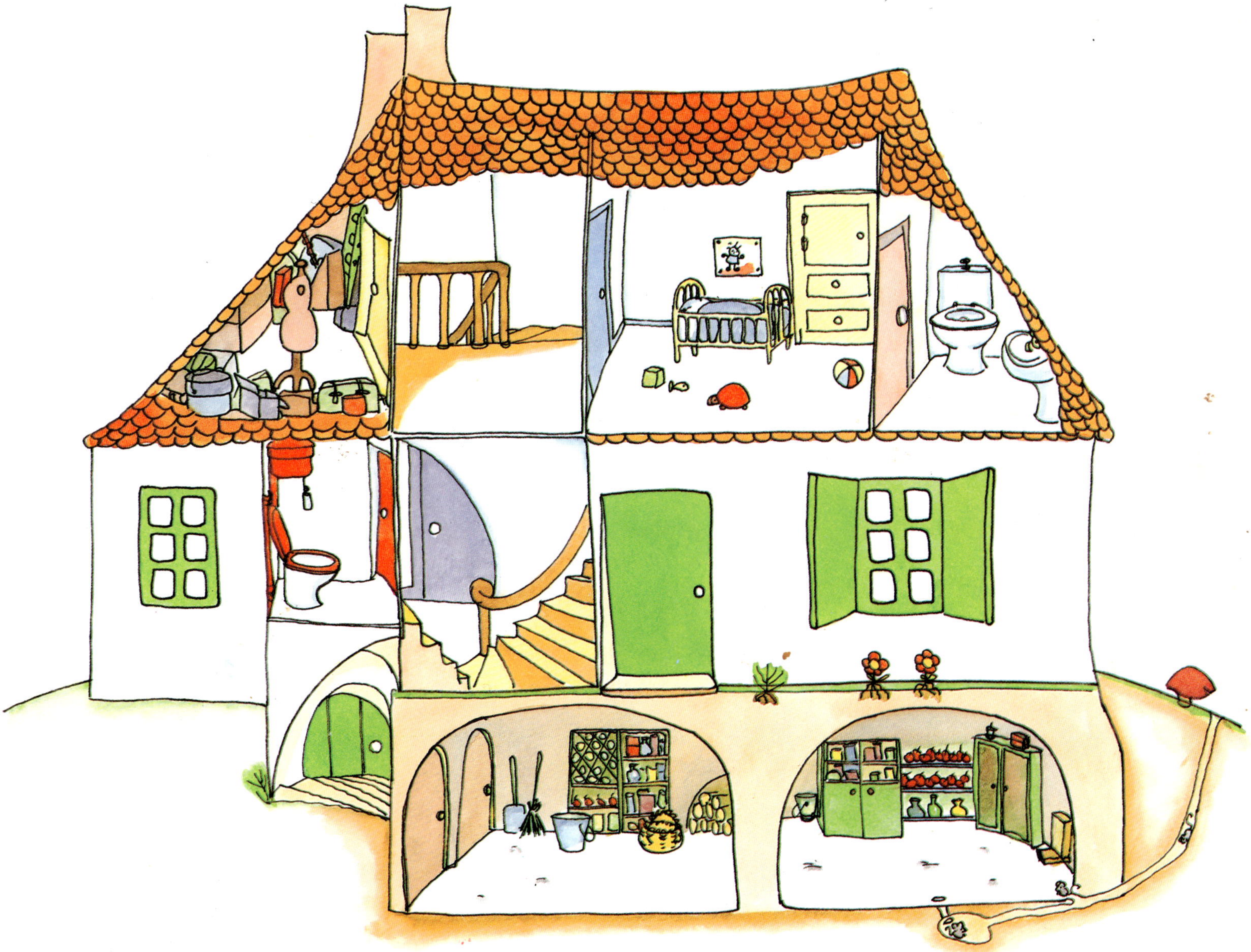

This is the big wooden door which always sticks and never seems to want to open.

But, today, Emily has her magic torch.

She stands in front of the big wooden door and says,

Abracadabra!

The door creaks open, and Emily goes into...

...the cellar

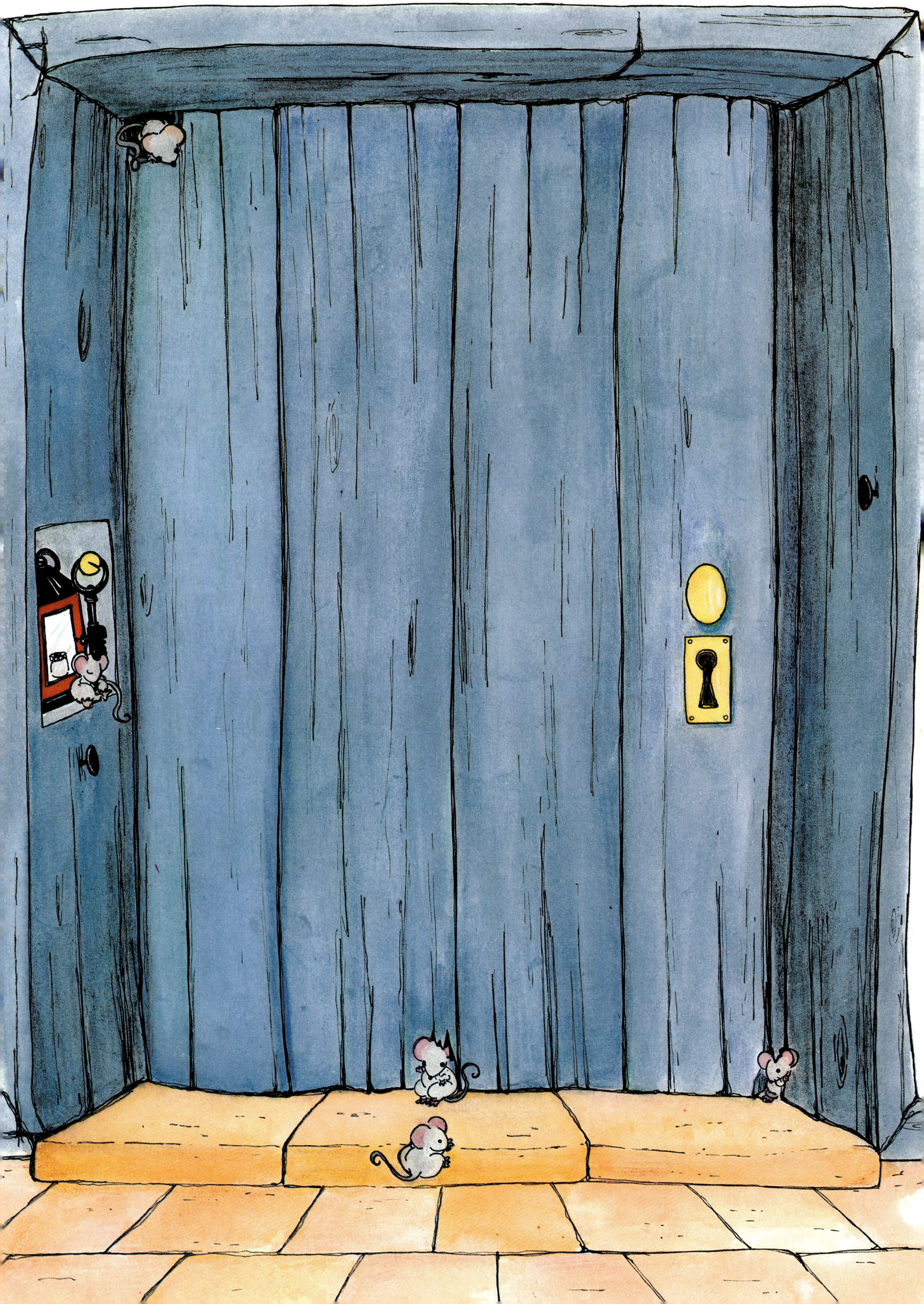

the cellar

The cellar is frightening.

Emily and Stephen go all the way down the steps.

It's dark,

and there are strange noises,

and a funny smell, like mushrooms.	It must be the monster!
Mind we don't wake him.	Sshh! Don't make a sound.

Oh no! The monster is awake.

Help! He's going to eat us.
Quick! Let's run for it!

This is the big wooden door which always sticks and never seems to want to open.

But, today, Emily has her magic torch.

She stands in front of the big wooden door and says,

Abracadabra!

The door creaks open, and Emily goes into...

...the kitchen

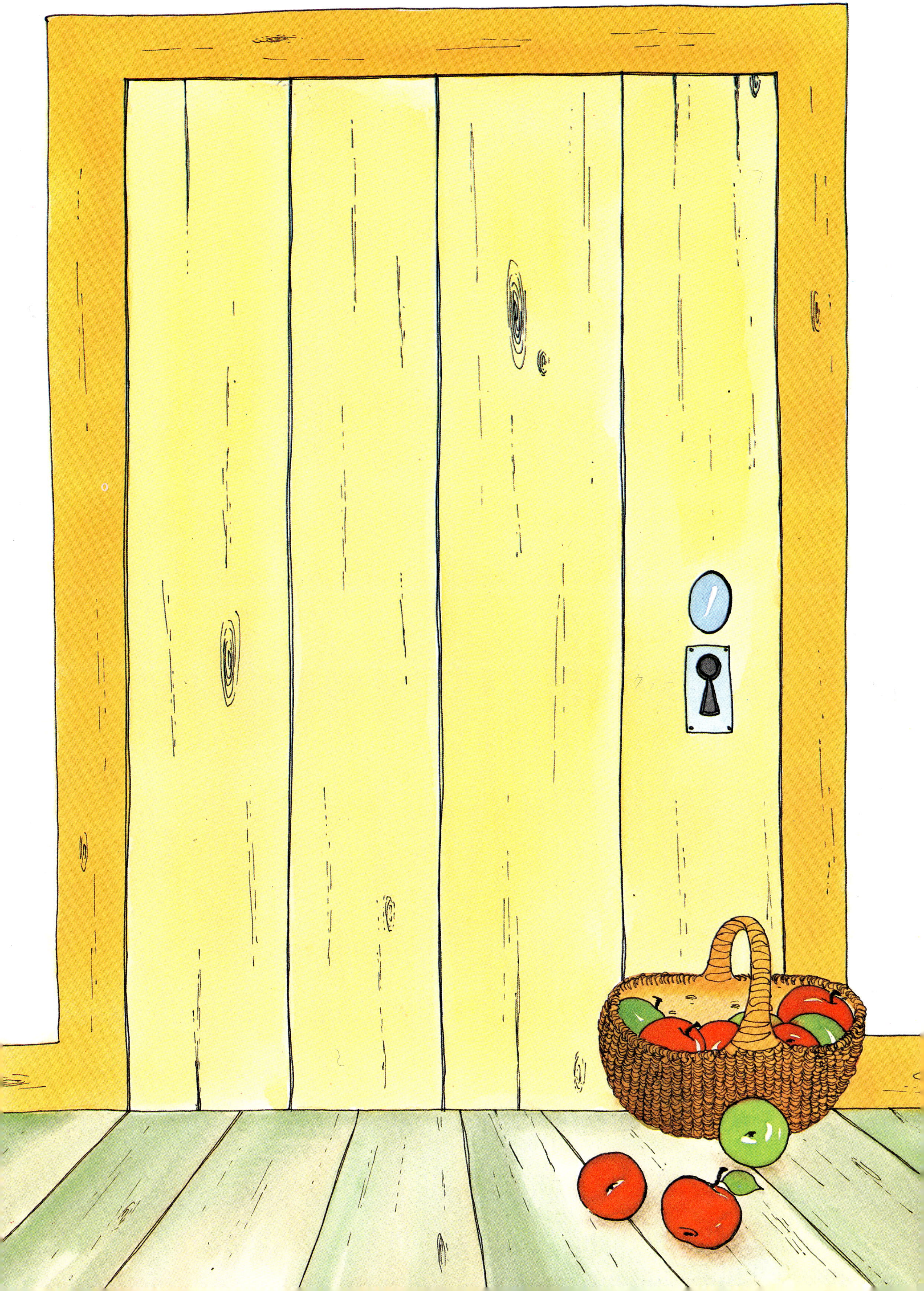

the kitchen

Mmmm! What a lovely smell.

I wonder where it's coming from?

I shall find out with my magic torch.

I look in the pots and pans,

and in all the jars...

Silly Emily!

I don't need a torch to know where that lovely smell is coming from. It's coming from the oven

and it is a great big cake.

But, look! It's burning.

Quick! Mummy! Daddy! The cake is burning.

There! You see, my torch saved the cake.

This is the big wooden door which always sticks and never seems to want to open.

But, today, Emily has her magic torch.

She stands in front of the big wooden door and says,

Abracadabra!

The door creaks open, and Emily goes into...

...the living room

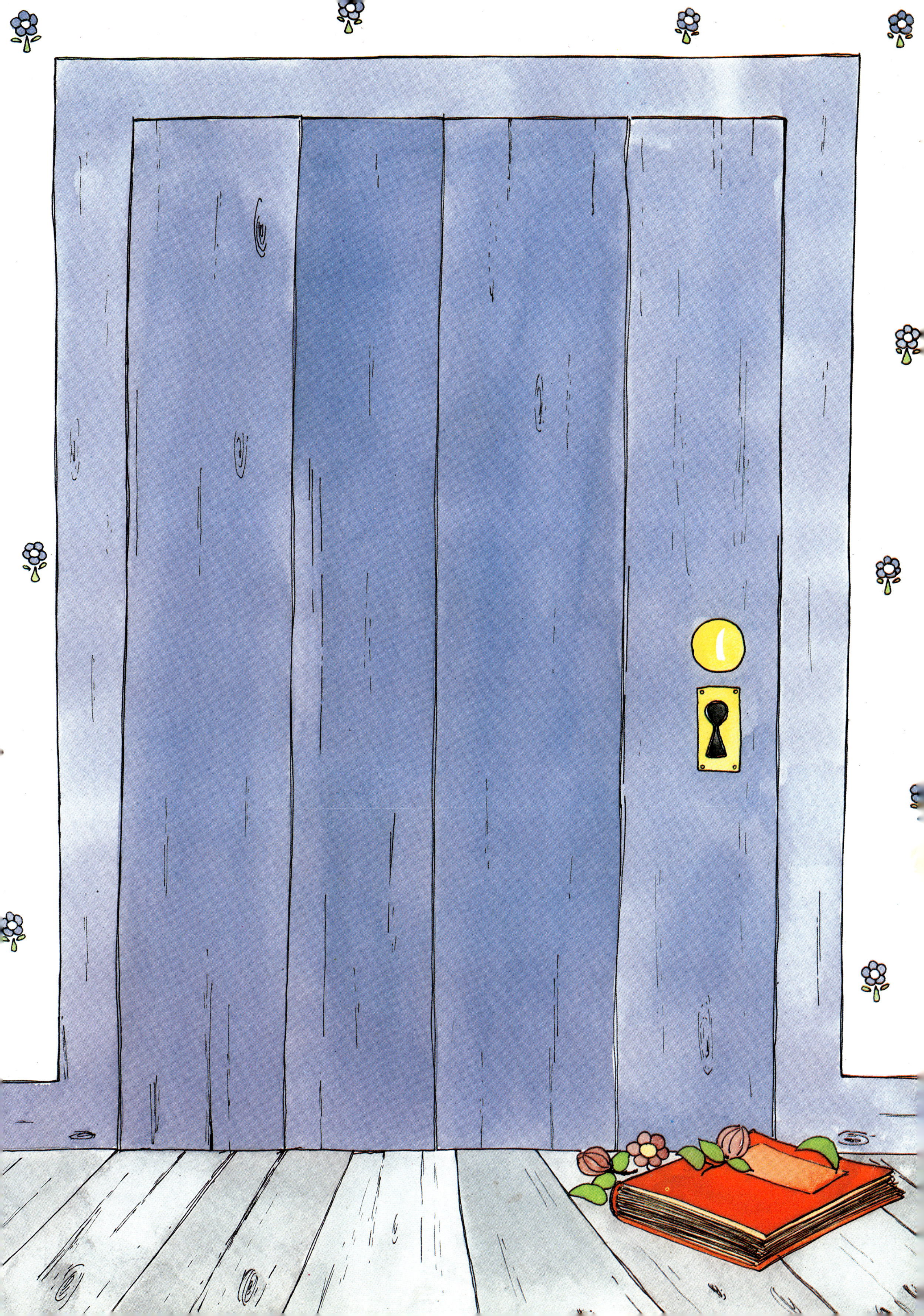

the living room

Oh dear! says Daddy. I've lost my pen. Emily and Stephen, will you help me look for it?

I shall find it with my magic torch.

In the wastepaper basket, I find a rubber.

Under the table, I find a button.

In the flowerpot, a rubber band.

On the bookshelf, a piece of string.

And behind the door, Arthur.

Daddy, I have looked simply everywhere

but I still can't find your pen.

Oh, sorry! says Daddy. It was in the bottom of my pocket all the time.

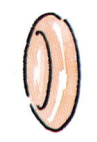

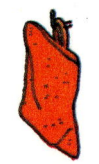

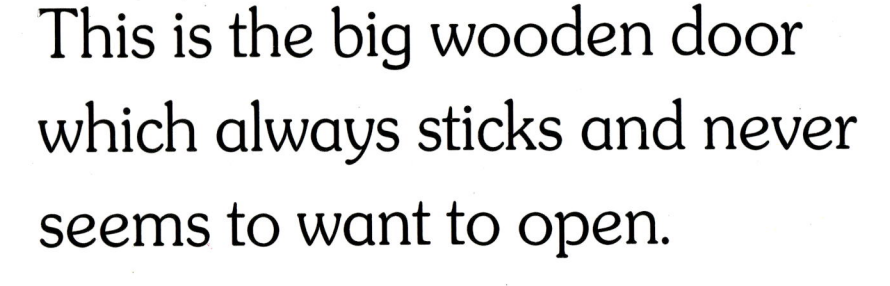

This is the big wooden door which always sticks and never seems to want to open.

But, today, Emily has her magic torch.

She stands in front of the big wooden door and says,

Abracadabra!

The door creaks open, and Emily goes into...

...the bathroom

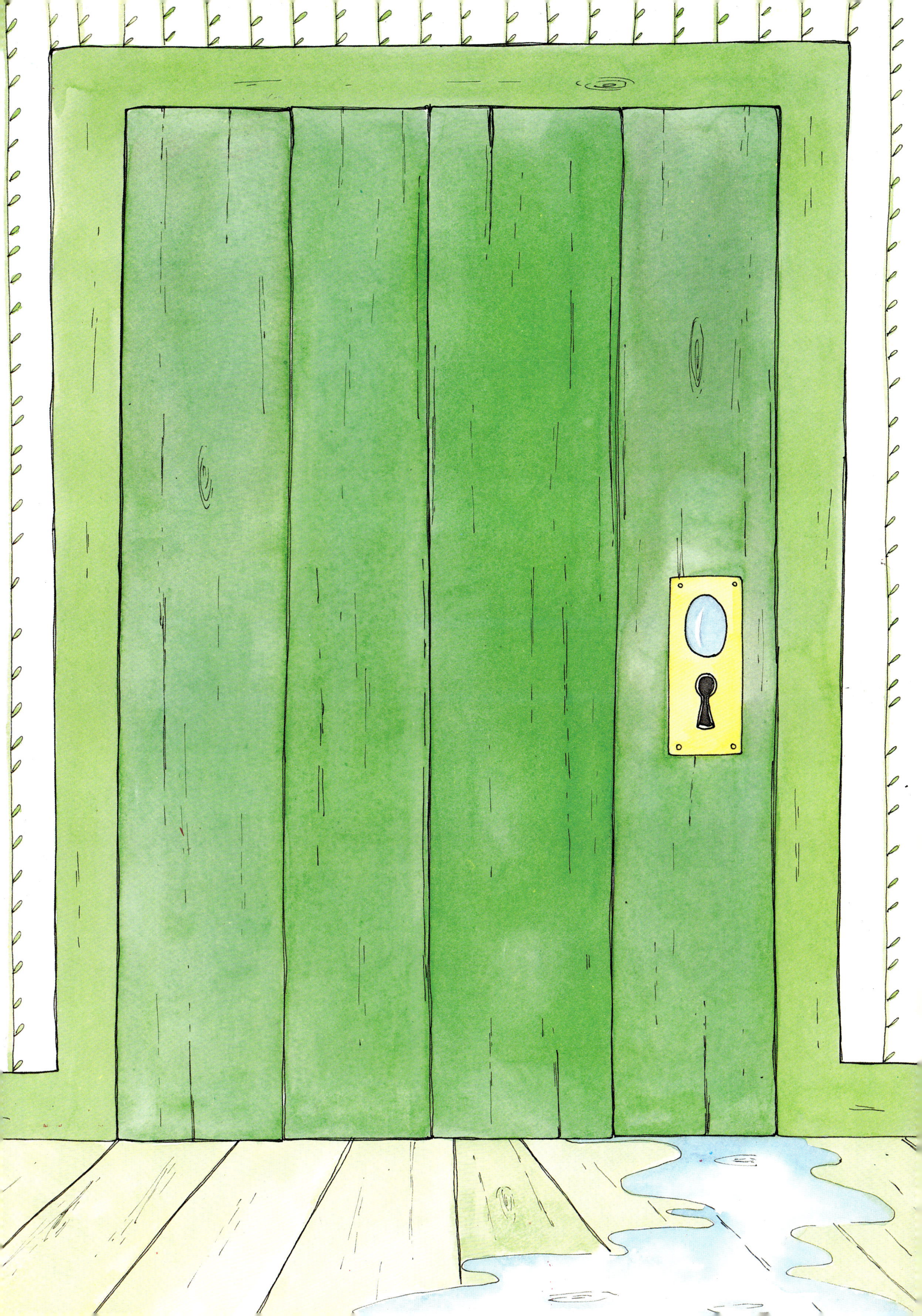

the bathroom

Poor Daddy! He never remembers to fix anything.

Look, he still hasn't mended the leaking pipe.

Perhaps he can't find the hole.

Well, I shall find it with my magic torch.

It will be easy. I just follow the pipe and look at it carefully.

Phew! Working makes you hot!

I must have a drink of water.

Good. Now I can carry on.

Hooray! I've found the leak.

Oh, Emily! That's not a leak. You've forgotten to turn off the tap!

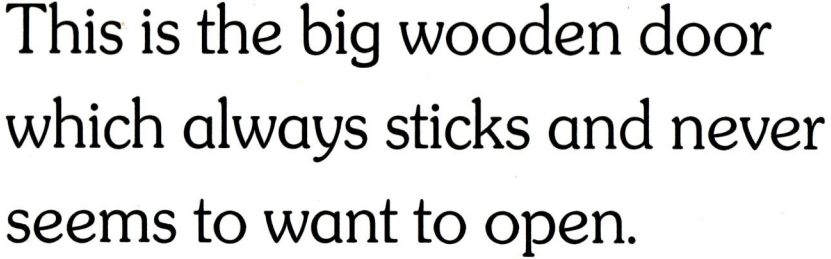

This is the big wooden door which always sticks and never seems to want to open.

But, today, Emily has her magic torch.

She stands in front of the big wooden door and says,

Abracadabra!

The door creaks open, and Emily goes into...

...the bedroom

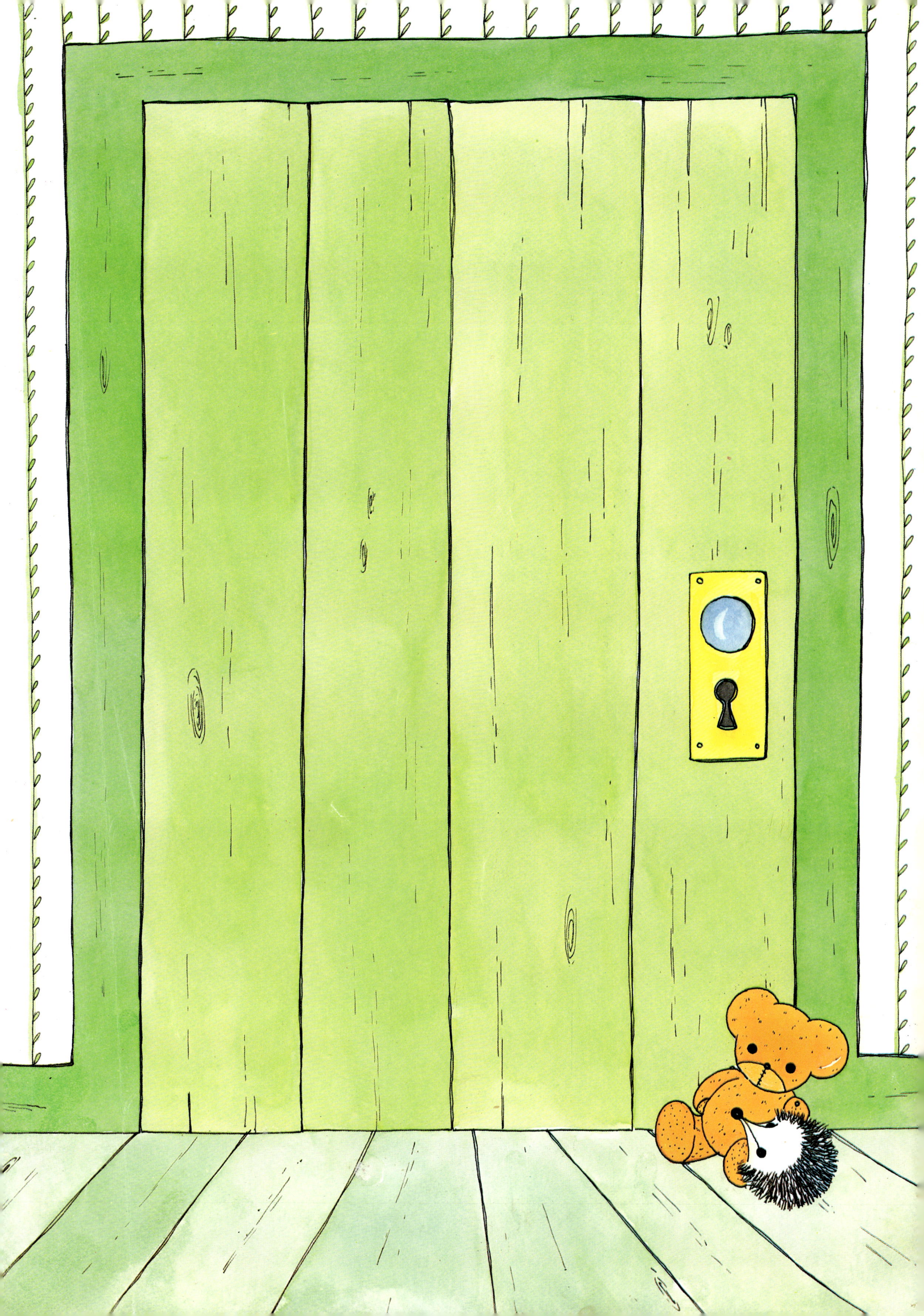

the bedroom

Oh dear, Emily. Your bedroom is in a mess.

No, it's not. Everything is as I like it,

with a few toys here, a few there,

and a few more over there.

In fact, I can walk across my bedroom with my eyes closed, without knocking over a single toy.

I'm sure that it will be easy with my magic torch.

Hop, and hop,
and hop, and . . .

Oops!

See, you can't do it, Emily.

But the chair doesn't count. It's not a toy!

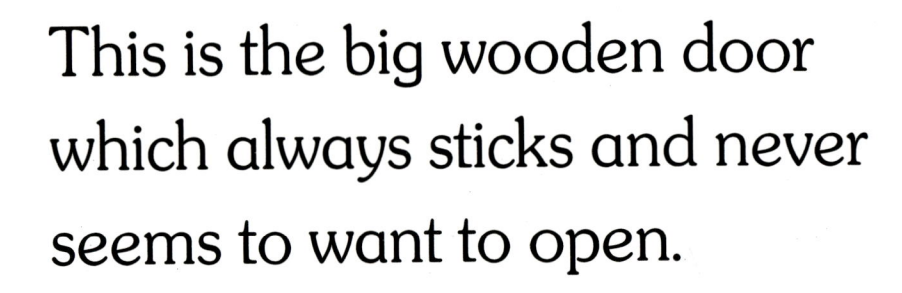

This is the big wooden door which always sticks and never seems to want to open.

But, today, Emily has her magic torch.

She stands in front of the big wooden door and says,

Abracadabra!

The door creaks open, and Emily goes into...

...the attic

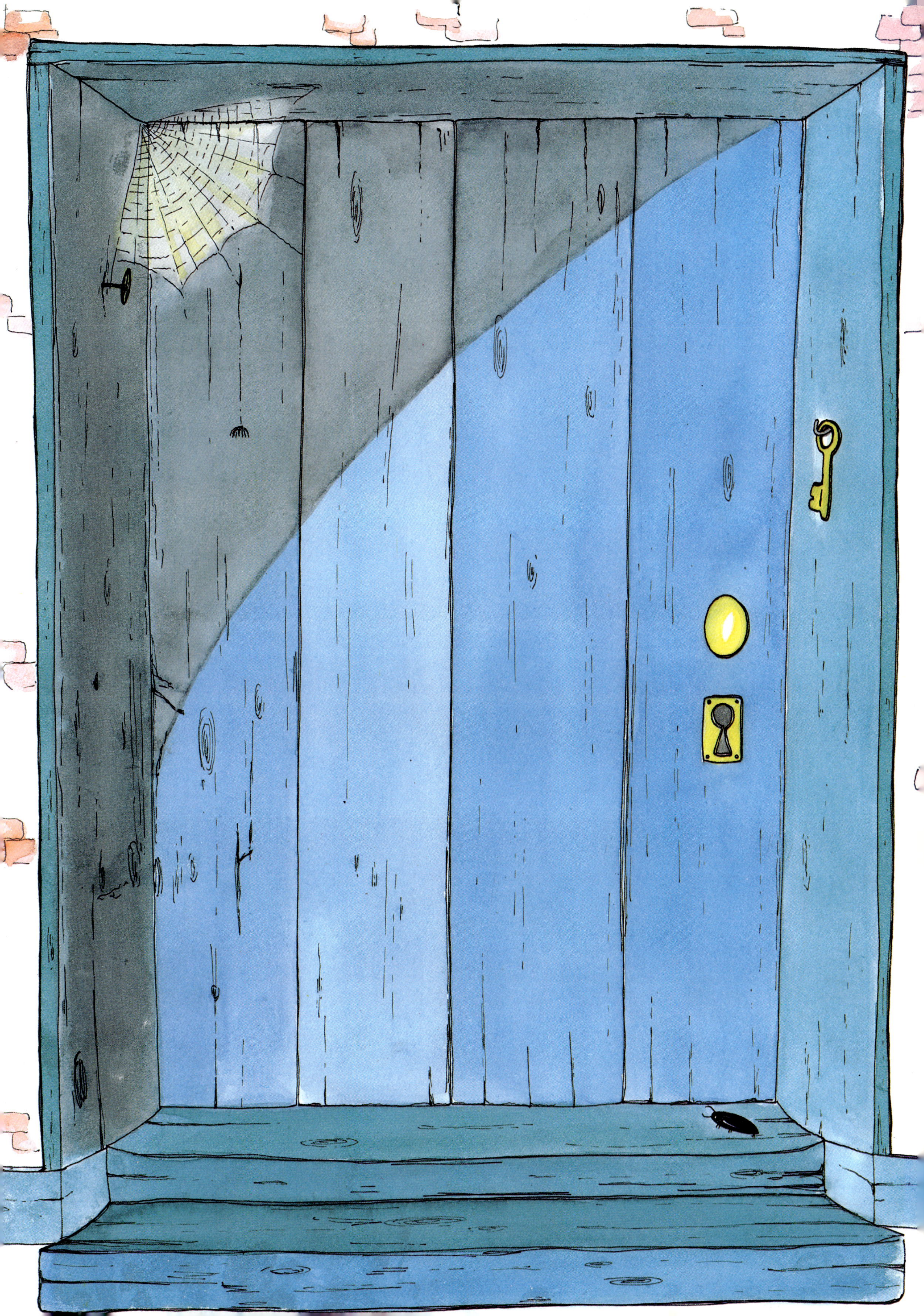

the attic

Mummy says that there's always
a lot of treasure in attics.

So let's find
some then.

But I cannot see
anything at all,

except old boxes, dust, cobwebs, and...

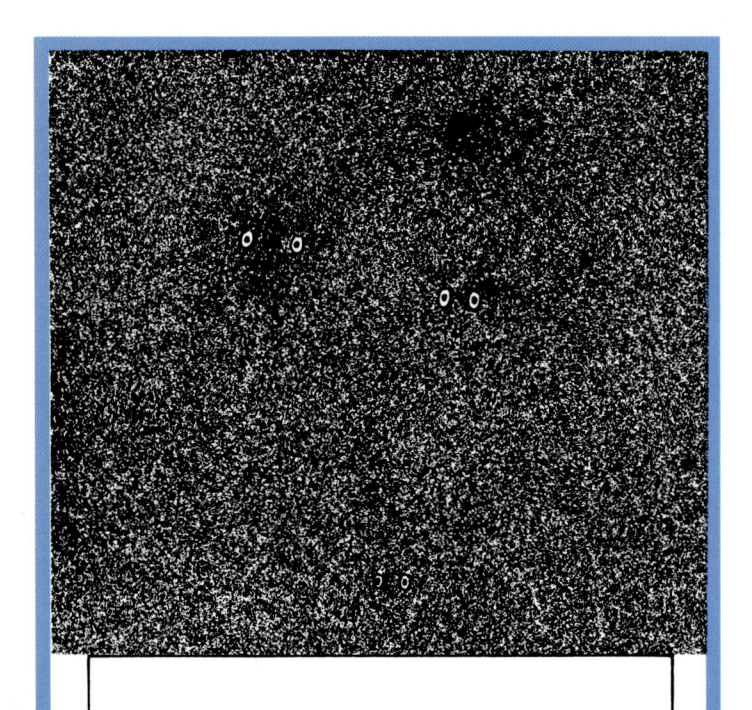

Help! It's gone all dark.

What's going on? say Mummy and Daddy.

It's my torch. It won't work any more.

Mummy says: That's because you didn't listen to us, and now your batteries have run out… and it is getting dark.

Never mind, I don't need a torch at night, because that's when I go to sleep.

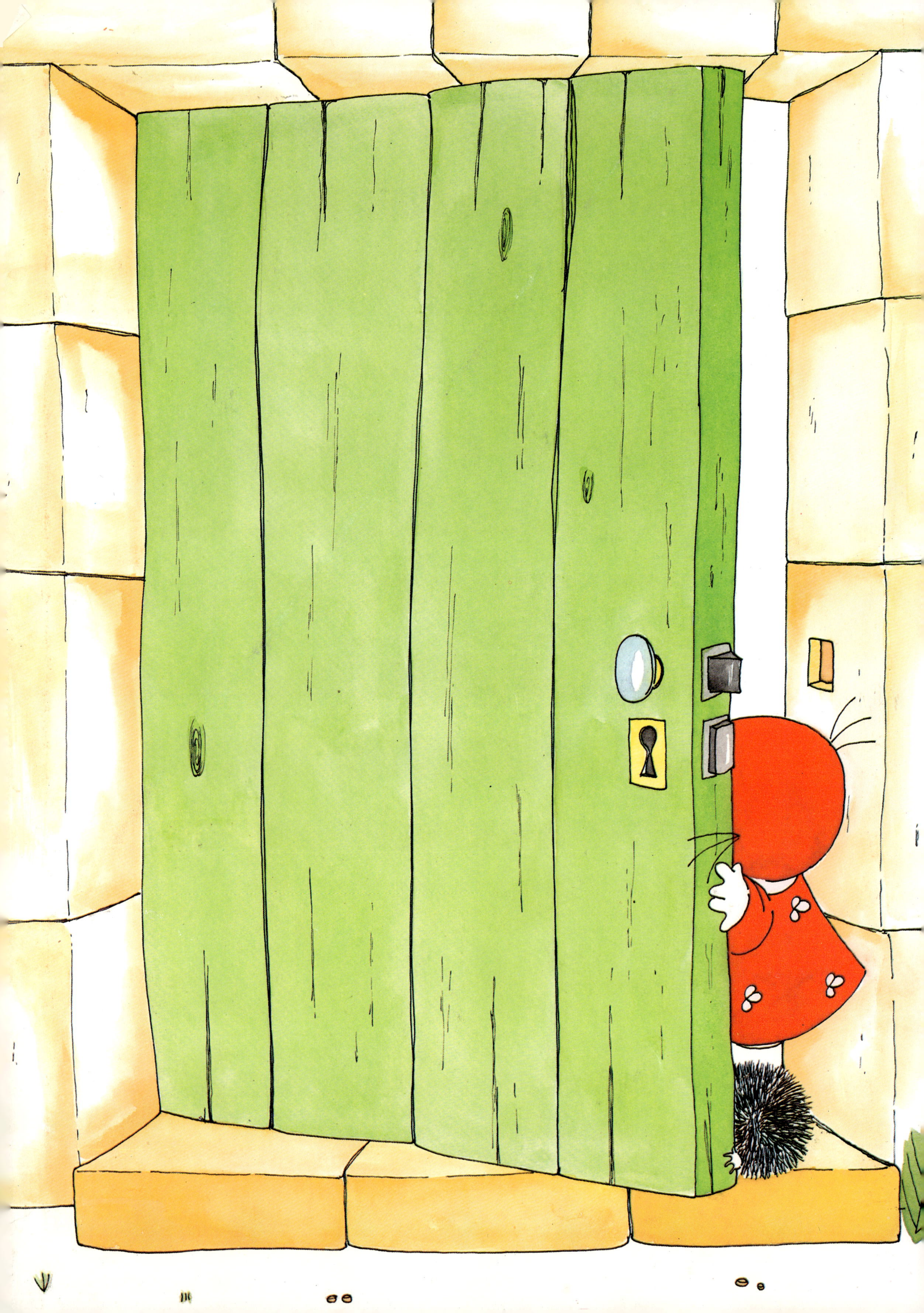